American Symbols

Uncle Sam

by Debbie L. Yanuck

Consultant:
Melodie Andrews, Ph.D.
Associate Professor of Early American History
Minnesota State University, Mankato

Capstone
press

Mankato, Minnesota

Capstone Press
151 Good Counsel Drive, P.O. Box 669, Mankato, Minnesota 56002
http://www.capstone-press.com

Library of Congress Cataloging-in-Publication Data
Yanuck, Debbie L.
 Uncle Sam / by Debbie L. Yanuck.
 p. cm.—(American symbols)
 Includes bibliographical references (p. 24) and index.
 Contents: Uncle Sam fast facts—American symbol of government—Samuel Wilson—
Uncle Sam becomes a symbol—Uncle Sam cartoons—Uncle Sam's look—"I WANT
YOU"—Uncle Sam today—Timeline—Hands on: draw Uncle Sam.
 ISBN 0-7368-2295-X (hardcover)
 1. Uncle Sam (Symbolic character)—Juvenile literature. 2. Wilson, Samuel, 1766–1854—
Juvenile literature. 3. United States—Biography—Juvenile literature. [1. Uncle Sam
(Symbolic character) 2. Wilson, Samuel, 1766–1854.] I. Title. II. Series.
E179 .Y29 2004
398.2'973'02—dc21
                                                                          2002156499

Editorial Credits
Roberta Schmidt, editor; Linda Clavel, designer; Kelly Garvin, photo researcher;
 Eric Kudalis and Karen Risch, product planning editors

Photo Credits
By permission of Gary Varvel and Creators Syndicate Inc., 19
Capstone Press/Linda Clavel, 9
Corbis/Philip Gould, 5; George Contorakes, 7; Bettmann, 15 (left), Joseph Sohm,
 ChromoSohm Inc., 18
Getty Images/Hulton Archive, 17
Library of Congress, 11, 13, 15 (right), 20
Stock Montage Inc., cover, 21

Table of Contents

Uncle Sam Fast Facts

* Uncle Sam is a symbol of the U.S. government.

* Uncle Sam is based on a man named Samuel Wilson. Wilson sold food to the U.S. Army during the War of 1812 (1812–1814).

* In September 1813, the name "Uncle Sam" appeared in a newspaper for the first time.

* James Montgomery Flagg painted the most famous picture of Uncle Sam in 1917.

* Uncle Sam's image can be found in many places. People make drawings of Uncle Sam. Some people dress up like Uncle Sam.

American Symbol of Government

Uncle Sam is a nickname for the U.S. government. Some people dress up like Uncle Sam. Other people draw pictures of him. Uncle Sam has a white beard and striped pants. He wears a top hat decorated with stars and stripes.

nickname
a name used with or instead of a real name

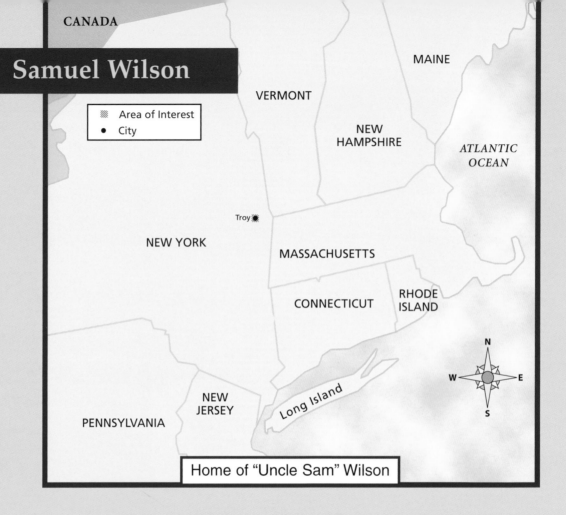

Samuel Wilson

CANADA

MAINE

VERMONT

NEW HAMPSHIRE

ATLANTIC OCEAN

Area of Interest

• City

Troy

NEW YORK

MASSACHUSETTS

CONNECTICUT

RHODE ISLAND

NEW JERSEY

Long Island

PENNSYLVANIA

N
W E
S

Home of "Uncle Sam" Wilson

Uncle Sam was based on a man named Samuel Wilson. Wilson lived in Troy, New York. Many people called him "Uncle Sam." During the War of 1812 (1812–1814),

Wilson sold meat to the U.S. Army. Each
barrel of Wilson's meat had the letters
"U.S." stamped on it. Soldiers started to
call the food "Uncle Sam's."

Uncle Sam Becomes a Symbol

In 1813, a reporter wrote a story about Wilson and his "U.S." meat. The story was printed in many newspapers. People started to call anything from the U.S. government "Uncle Sam's." Uncle Sam became a symbol for the government.

11

Uncle Sam Cartoons

In the 1830s, people began to draw cartoons of Uncle Sam. These pictures were printed in newspapers. They showed how people felt about the U.S. government. Many cartoons made fun of U.S. laws and actions. Other cartoons supported the U.S. government.

Uncle Sam

1834 cartoon

Uncle Sam's Look

Uncle Sam's look changed over the years. He started to wear a top hat and tailcoat in the mid-1800s. This costume copied a circus clown named Dan Rice. Early drawings showed Uncle Sam as a young man. Cartoonist Thomas Nast made his hair and beard gray in 1869.

cartoonist
a person who draws cartoons

early Uncle Sam cartoon

Thomas Nast cartoon

15

"I WANT YOU"

In 1917, James Montgomery Flagg painted the most famous picture of Uncle Sam. His poster asked men to join the U.S. Army. It showed Uncle Sam pointing his finger. The words on the poster read, "I WANT YOU."

NT YOU
U.S. ARMY
EST RECRUITING STATION

James Montgomery Flagg - 1918

Uncle Sam Today

Uncle Sam is an important symbol today. On the Fourth of July, people dress up as Uncle Sam and lead parades.

People still draw cartoons of Uncle Sam to share their feelings about the United States. Uncle Sam is a symbol of the U.S. government.

Timeline

1766—Samuel Wilson is born.

1813—"Uncle Sam" is mentioned in a newspaper article for the first time.

1830s—People start to draw cartoons of Uncle Sam.

1854—Samuel Wilson dies.

1917—James Montgomery Flagg paints the most famous portrait of Uncle Sam.

1961—U.S. Congress passes a resolution that hails "Uncle Sam" Wilson of Troy, New York, as the father of the national symbol.

Hands On: Draw Uncle Sam

Create your own Uncle Sam cartoon. How would he look today? How would he be dressed?

What You Need

White paper
Colored pencils
Friends

What You Do

1. Think of how you picture the United States and Uncle Sam. How do you think Uncle Sam should look? Should he wear a top hat? Should he have a white beard? What type of shirt should he wear?
2. Use colored pencils to draw your own cartoon of Uncle Sam.
3. Show your picture to your friends.

Compare your drawings. What did you draw the same? What did you draw differently?

Words to Know

government (GUHV-urn-muhnt)—the people and laws that rule a country

nickname (NIK-name)—a name used with or instead of a real name

soldier (SOLE-jur)—a person who is in the military

symbol (SIM-buhl)—an object that stands for something else

tailcoat (TAYL-koht)—a man's black coat that has a long, rounded, split tail

Read More

Marcovitz, Hal. *Uncle Sam.* American Symbols and Their Meanings. Philadelphia: Mason Crest Publishers, 2003.

West, Delno C., and Jean M. West. *Uncle Sam and Old Glory: Symbols of America.* New York: Atheneum Books, 2000.

Internet Sites

Do you want to find out more about Uncle Sam? Let FactHound, our fact-finding hound dog, do the research for you.

Here's how:

1) Visit *http://www.facthound.com*

2) Type in the **Book ID** number:
   073682295X

3) Click on **FETCH IT**.

FactHound will fetch Internet sites picked by our editors just for you!

Index